MY AMERICAN STORY

OUR TRADITIONS

JUNE 19

WHAT SYMBOLS AND CELEBRATIONS DO AMERICANS SHARE?

DK | Penguin Random House

Editorial Management by Oriel Square
Produced for DK by Collaborate Agency
Index by James Helling

Author Jennifer Kaul
Series Editor Megan DuVarney Forbes
Publisher Nick Hunter
Publisher Sarah Forbes
Publishing Project Manager Katherine Neep
Production Controller Isabell Schart
Picture Researcher Nunhoih Guite
Production Editor Shanker Prasad

First American Edition, 2023
Published in the United States by DK Publishing
1745 Broadway, 20th Floor, New York, NY 10019

Copyright © 2023 Dorling Kindersley Limited
DK, a Division of Penguin Random House LLC
19 20 21 22 23 10 9 8 7 6 5 4 3 2 1
001–334893–Oct/2023

A catalog record for this book
is available from the Library of Congress.
ISBN 978-0-7440-7768-1

DK books are available at special discounts when purchased
in bulk for sales promotions, premiums, fund-raising, or educational use.
For details, contact: DK Publishing Special Markets,
1745 Broadway, 20th Floor, New York, NY 10019
SpecialSales@dk.com

Printed and bound in China

The publisher would like to thank the following for their kind permission to reproduce their images:
(Key: a-above; b-below/bottom; c-center; f-far; l-left; r-right; t-top)

5 Getty Images / iStock: Jganz (tr). **6 Alamy Stock Photo:** Lana Sundman (cl). **7 Alamy Stock Photo:** Martin Bennett (tl). **8 Getty Images:** Bettmann (cr). **9 National Portrait Gallery, Smithsonian Institution:** gift of the Morris and Gwendolyn Cafritz Foundation (bl). **Shutterstock.com:** FloridaStock (crb). **10 Library of Congress, Washington, D.C.:** LC-DIG-ppmsca-44470/Constitution of the United States, Grant. , 1865. [Philadelphia: Publisher Not Transcribed] Photograph. https://www.loc.gov/item/2018695121/. (br). **11 Dreamstime.com:** Alberto Dubini (cr). **13 Dreamstime.com:** F11photo (t). **Getty Images / iStock:** E+ / dszc (bl). **14 Alamy Stock Photo:** Danita Delimont / Walter Bibikow (clb). **Dreamstime.com:** Petr Svec (b). **15 Library of Congress, Washington, D.C.:** LC-DIG-ppmsca-23759 / Latrobe, Benjamin Henry, 1764-1820, architect (tl). **17 Getty Images:** Bettmann (cla). **18 Getty Images / iStock:** DigitalVision Vectors / clu (bl). **19 Dreamstime.com:** Kalyan V. Srinivas (l). **20 Alamy Stock Photo:** Bob Daemmrich (cl). **21 Alamy Stock Photo:** Mark Reinstein (c). **22 Alamy Stock Photo:** Robert Landau (b). **23 Library of Congress, Washington, D.C.:** LC-DIG-ppmsc-03521 / Flagg, James Montgomery, 1877-1960, artist (bl). **24 Alamy Stock Photo:** Ken Gillespie Photography (br). **25 Getty Images / iStock:** E+ / Miodrag Ignjatovic (br). **27 Getty Images:** Bettmann (br). **28 Dreamstime.com:** Olga Mendenhall (br). **29 Alamy Stock Photo:** IanDagnall Computing (tl); PAINTING (br). **30 Alamy Stock Photo:** Allen Creative / Steve Allen (cr). **31 Dreamstime.com:** Kmiragaya (cr). **32 Alamy Stock Photo:** UPI (cla). **Dreamstime.com:** Vadimrysev (br). **Getty Images / iStock:** Bastiaan Slabbers (bl). **33 Getty Images:** Paul Moseley / Fort Worth Star-Telegram / Tribune News Service (cr). **Library of Congress, Washington, D.C.:** LC-DIG-pga-02797 / Strobridge & Co. Lith. (tl). **34 Alamy Stock Photo:** Planetpix / Richard Ellis (bl). **Getty Images / iStock:** E+ / Toshe_O (br). **Getty Images:** George Rose (crb). **35 Library of Congress, Washington, D.C.:** LC-DIG-ppmsca-59409/Declaration of Independence and its signers. , ca. 1906. [United States:publisher not transcribed] Photograph. https://www.loc.gov/item/2018757145/. (br). **36 Getty Images:** Archive Photos / Stock Montage (br). **Getty Images / iStock:** Photoboyko (bl). **37 Getty Images / iStock:** E+ / AzmanL (br). **38 Alamy Stock Photo:** REUTERS / Pu Ying Huang (b). **40 Alamy Stock Photo:** Glasshouse Images / JT Vintage (b). **41 Alamy Stock Photo:** B Christopher (clb). **Getty Images:** Tetra images / Inti St Clair (tr). **43 Getty Images / iStock:** TD Dolci (cra). **45 Dreamstime.com:** Chon Kit Leong (tr). **47 Alamy Stock Photo:** Bob Daemmrich (cr). **Dreamstime.com:** Alberto Dubini (tr). **Getty Images / iStock:** TD Dolci (br)

All other images © Dorling Kindersley Limited

Illustrations by: Karen Saavedra

For the curious
www.dk.com

MIX
Paper | Supporting
responsible forestry
FSC™ C018179

This book was made with Forest
Stewardship Council™ certified
paper – one small step in DK's
commitment to a sustainable future.
**For more information go to
www.dk.com/our-green-pledge**

CONTENTS

WHAT IS A SYMBOL?

Imagine that you are walking down a street when you see a bright red sign shaped like an octagon. What do you do? Even if you cannot read the word written across this sign, you likely know to stop. A stop sign is a well-known **symbol** that keeps people safe when traveling along a road.

A SYMBOL IS SOMETHING, OFTEN A SHAPE OR PICTURE, THAT STANDS FOR SOMETHING ELSE.

Symbols are everywhere. They are on road signs to help people know how to drive. They appear as icons on electronic screens to help people use their devices. They are on waste bins to help people know where to put their trash and recyclables. Symbols are used by companies to help people notice their products. Symbols communicate ideas or messages to people without using language.

AMERICAN ★ SYMBOLS ★

America has a lot of symbols. These symbols help the country function and make Americans feel proud. Some American symbols are the American flag and the Pledge of Allegiance. When people see or hear these symbols, they think about the strength and justice of their country as well as its history, both good and bad.

WHAT IS A TRADITION?

A TRADITION IS A BELIEF OR CUSTOM THAT IS PASSED DOWN FROM GENERATION TO GENERATION. MANY SYMBOLS ARE PART OF THE AMERICAN TRADITION. THEY WERE CREATED OR CHOSEN LONG AGO AND HAVE BEEN A PART OF AMERICAN LIFE FOR A LONG TIME, ALTHOUGH TRADITIONS ALSO CHANGE OVER TIME. THESE SYMBOLS HELP PEOPLE UNDERSTAND THEIR GOVERNMENT AND CELEBRATE THEIR COUNTRY.

THE AMERICAN FLAG

★ ★ ★ ★ ★ ★ ★ ★ ★ ★ ★ ★ ★ ★ ★ ★ ★ ★ ★ ★

When Americans fought for their **independence** from Great Britain, they needed a new flag. On June 14, 1777, the Flag Resolution said what America's flag should look like. It said the flag would "be made of thirteen stripes, alternate red and white; that the union be thirteen stars, white in a blue field, **representing** a new Constellation".

THE AMERICAN FLAG WAS CREATED AS A SYMBOL OF FREEDOM.

The original flag had 13 stars, one for each of America's original colonies. As more states were added to the union, or country, more stars were added to the flag. The American flag now has 50 stars for its 50 states. Its 13 stripes continue to represent the first 13 colonies of the U.S. No one knows for sure who made the first American flag. However, some people believe that it was designed by Francis Hopkinson and sewn by Betsy Ross. Another name for the American flag is Old Glory.

RED, WHITE, AND BLUE

The colors on the flag are meant to represent values that are important to America:

- red stands for bravery
- white stands for purity
- blue stands for perseverance and justice.

HOW TO DISPLAY THE ★ AMERICAN FLAG ★

There are many rules for how to show respect when flying the American flag. For example, the flag should be flown at half-mast, or half way down the flag pole, when the nation is mourning. A flag should not be flown in weather that could damage it, and it should not touch the ground.

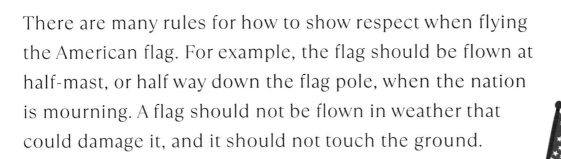

THE BALD EAGLE

★ ★

On June 20, 1782, the Continental Congress of the 13 original states approved a design for the Great Seal of the United States. The bald eagle was a part of the design. The eagle had been a symbol of strength for thousands of years throughout the world.

The eagle on the seal is considered to be "on the wing & rising". It has a shield with stars and stripes on its breast. It holds an olive branch in its right talon and a set of 13 arrows in its left talon. The eagle's head is always turned toward the right. This shows that America prefers peace but is willing and able to defend itself.

THE EAGLE AS AN ★ AMERICAN SYMBOL ★

The national seal is used in many important places. For example, it is used on documents signed by the president. It is also used by other government officers. It is located on people's passports and the back of the one-dollar bill. By law, it can only be used by the U.S. government.

BALD EAGLES IN AMERICA

The bald eagle lives only in North America. It is often found near rivers and lakes. It preys upon fish, birds, small mammals, and reptiles such as turtles and snakes. The population of eagles has decreased since 1782 because of human actions. Hunters have killed eagles. The use of the pesticide DDT made it difficult for young eagles to develop in their eggs. The use of DDT was banned in 1972, and the bald eagle was made an endangered species in 1978. Since then, the eagle population has increased from less than 450 nesting pairs to over 6,000.

BENJAMIN FRANKLIN WAS ONE OF THE FOUNDING FATHERS INVOLVED IN DESIGNING THE NATIONAL SEAL.

THE CONSTITUTION

On September 17, 1787, America's **constitution** was signed into law. It was written by 55 delegates. These men were chosen to make decisions for the people of their states. They set out to create a government that would be strong enough to protect its people from other countries. At the same time, they did not want a government so powerful it could limit individual rights.

The Constitution is one of the oldest written forms of government in the world, and it acts as a symbol of American democracy. The Constitution gives all powers not directly given to the **federal** government to state governments. It allows **amendments**, or changes, to be made to its laws. It also includes the Bill of Rights. Despite the changes that can be made, the Constitution is also a symbol of consistency. Our rights always stay the same under the Constitution, no matter who the president is.

The Bill of Rights lists rights guaranteed for all American citizens. The first five of these ten amendments protect the following rights:

- First Amendment: protects the right to freedom of speech and freedom of religion

- Second Amendment: protects the right to keep and carry weapons

- Third Amendment: stops the government from requiring people to house soldiers

- Fourth Amendment: stops the government from searching someone's home without a reason

- Fifth Amendment: protects people accused of crimes.

★ BRANCHES OF GOVERNMENT

The Constitution created a federal government with three branches of power. These branches are meant to keep each other in check so no one group or person becomes too powerful. The branches are:

- The Legislative Branch: Congress

- The Executive Branch: The president

- The Judicial Branch: The Supreme Court.

THE

LIBERTY BELL

★ ★

In 1751, Pennsylvania bought a large bell to hang in the state house, later renamed Independence Hall. Unfortunately, it was cracked while being tested. The bell was melted and recast, or formed again.

This bell, the Liberty Bell, was used to call people together. It called lawmakers for meetings and townspeople for announcements. The bell weighs 2,080 pounds and is 12 feet around at its base. It has the words "Proclaim liberty throughout all the land unto all the inhabitants thereof" on it.

THE LIBERTY BELL WAS RUNG ON JULY 8, 1776 TO CELEBRATE THE FIRST PUBLIC READING OF THE DECLARATION OF INDEPENDENCE.

★ INDEPENDENCE HALL ★

Independence Hall is an important place in American history. It is where the Declaration of Independence was signed in 1776. It is also where delegates wrote and signed the U.S. Constitution in 1787.

★ THE LIBERTY BELL'S CRACK ★

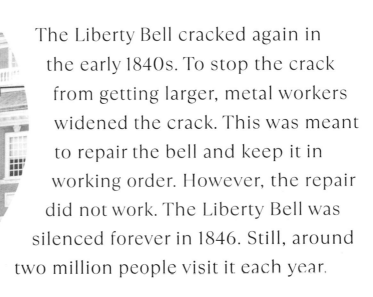

The Liberty Bell cracked again in the early 1840s. To stop the crack from getting larger, metal workers widened the crack. This was meant to repair the bell and keep it in working order. However, the repair did not work. The Liberty Bell was silenced forever in 1846. Still, around two million people visit it each year.

THE WHITE HOUSE

★ ★ ★ ★ ★ ★ ★ ★ ★ ★ ★ ★ ★ ★ ★ ★ ★ ★ ★ ★

In 1791, the U.S. government held a contest to design the house where the president would live. While kings and queens in other countries lived in grand palaces, the country's founders chose a simpler building for the president's home and office. A design created by architect James Hoban won. Construction began on October 13, 1792. The building was called the Executive Mansion until 1901 when it officially became known as the White House.

The second president, John Adams, was the first to live in the White House. Since then, every president has lived there during their presidency. The White House was burned down by the British during the War of 1812, but was then rebuilt. Changes were made over time by various presidents. The **Oval Office**, where the president works, was added in 1909.

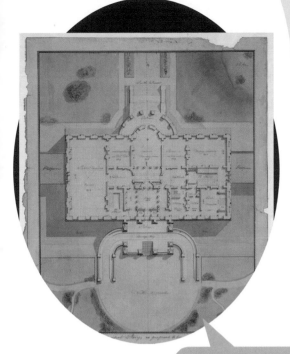

THE WHITE HOUSE TODAY

The White House is located at 1600 Pennsylvania Avenue N.W. in Washington, D.C. It covers 18 acres with six floors housing 132 rooms. It is the home and workplace of the president.

ORIGINAL WHITE HOUSE DESIGN DRAWING

VISITING THE WHITE HOUSE

The White House is the only **residence** of a country's leader that is open to the public free of charge. People who would like to visit the White House can register for a self-guided tour. There is also a White House Visitor Center that people can go to see.

DID YOU KNOW?

RECORDS SHOW THAT ENSLAVED PEOPLE FROM THE AREA AROUND WASHINGTON, D.C. WORKED ON BUILDING THE WHITE HOUSE AND OTHER IMPORTANT BUILDINGS SUCH AS THE CAPITOL.

THE NATIONAL ANTHEM

★ ★ ★ ★ ★ ★ ★ ★ ★ ★ ★ ★ ★ ★ ★ ★ ★ ★ ★ ★

On the morning of September 14, 1814, Francis Scott Key wrote what would become America's **national anthem**. He wrote it during the War of 1812, when the new nation of the U.S. was fighting against Great Britain. He was inspired by U.S. soldiers who raised the American flag over a fort that was being bombed by the British.

"The Star-Spangled Banner" became the official U.S. national anthem in 1931. "The Star-Spangled Banner" is still an important part of America today. The song expresses feelings of pride and **patriotism** in the U.S. These are feelings that Francis Scott Key most likely felt when he wrote the words hundreds of years ago.

According to the NAACP, an organization that fights racial inequality, the hymn "Lift Every Voice and Sing" is often considered "the Black National Anthem."

★ THE STAR-SPANGLED BANNER ★

The words to the U.S. National Anthem are:

"Oh, say can you see,

By the dawn's early light

What so proudly we hailed

At the twilight's last gleaming,

Whose broad stripes and bright stars,

Thru the perilous fight,

O'er the ramparts we watched

Were so gallantly streaming?

And the rockets red glare,

The bombs bursting in air,

Gave proof through the night

That our flag was still there.

O, say, does that

Star-Spangled Banner yet wave

O'er the land of the free

And the home of the brave?"

★ THE ANTHEM AT SPORTING EVENTS ★

The anthem was first connected with sports during the first game of the 1918 World Series. America was fighting in World War I at the time, and many people had died. When the U.S. Navy band played "The Star-Spangled Banner", people turned to face the flag. They put their hands over their hearts and sang along. The song was soon played at more and more sporting events until it became common. Athletes have sometimes protested "The Star-Spangled Banner". For example, professional football player Colin Kaepernick began kneeling during the song in 2016. He did this to protest police brutality against Black Americans.

THE STATUE OF LIBERTY

In 1875, a French sculptor began work on the Statue of Liberty. Frédéric-Auguste Bartholdi and his team worked on this **sculpture** until 1884. It was a gift from France to the U.S. to celebrate their friendship, 100 years after the country's founding.

The Statue of Liberty is a large statue of a woman. She is holding a torch, and a tablet with July 4, 1776 on it to symbolize America's independence. This is the date the Declaration of Independence was signed. There is a crown meant to symbolize the sun on the Statue of Liberty's head. A broken shackle and chains at her foot represent America's abolishment of slavery, which was recent at that time.

INSIDE THE CONSTRUCTION OF THE STATUE OF LIBERTY

CONSTRUCTION OF THE STATUE

The Statue of Liberty was taken apart so it could be shipped from France to America. It arrived in New York City in 1885. It has stood on Liberty Island ever since. The sculpture has a steel frame that was designed by Gustave Eiffel, the man who created France's Eiffel Tower. It is covered in 31 tons of copper sheets. While the Statue of Liberty was originally a copper color, it is now green because of exposure to the weather over time.

★ ELLIS ISLAND ★

ELLIS ISLAND IS LOCATED BETWEEN NEW YORK AND NEW JERSEY. IT IS WHERE MORE THAN 12 MILLION IMMIGRANTS ENTERED THE U.S. BY SHIP. ELLIS ISLAND WELCOMED IMMIGRANTS FROM 1892 UNTIL 1954.

THE STATUE OF LIBERTY, WITHOUT ITS PEDESTAL, IS OVER 151 FEET TALL AND 225 TONS IN WEIGHT.

The Statue of Liberty was a sign for immigrants that they had made it to America after a long journey across the ocean. A plaque on the Statue of Liberty reads:

"Give me your tired, your poor, your huddled masses yearning to breathe free, the wretched refuse of your teeming shore. Send these, the homeless, tempest-tost to me, I lift my lamp beside the golden door!"

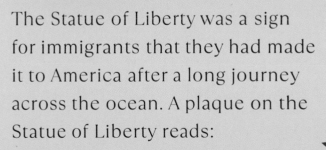

THE PLEDGE OF ALLEGIANCE

★ ★

On September 8, 1892, the **pledge** was first published. It was written by Francis Bellamy for a youth magazine. It was meant to celebrate the 400th anniversary of Christopher Columbus's arrival in the Americas.

The Pledge of Allegiance is a chance for people to show their patriotism. It became the country's official pledge in 1942. At this time, people started saying the pledge with their right hand over their heart. Before then, people had said the pledge while stretching their right hand out toward the flag. However, this was similar to the salute of the Nazis in Germany. The wording of the pledge was changed slightly over time. The Pledge of Allegiance is often said at the start of the day in public schools. It is also recited by Congress at the start of each day they are in session.

OLD VERSIONS OF THE PLEDGE

The first version read "I pledge allegiance to my Flag and the Republic for which it stands; one nation indivisible, with liberty and Justice for all". In 1924, the words "my flag" were replaced by "the flag of the United States of America". In 1954, President Eisenhower added the phrase "under God".

The current version of the Pledge of Allegiance is:

"I pledge allegiance to the flag of the United States of America and to the Republic for which it stands, one nation under God, indivisible, with liberty and justice for all."

OUR AMERICAN SYMBOLS

There are many official symbols of the U.S., but what does America mean to you? Many communities, families, and individuals have their own special symbols that stand for our country. These might include certain songs, foods, sports, and more.

Apple pie, fried chicken, and barbeque are often thought of as American foods. Jazz is one of many types of music that began in America. Sports such as baseball and football are also symbols of America for many people.

"AMERICA THE BEAUTIFUL"

"America the Beautiful" is one song that is symbolic of America. It was written by Katharine Lee Bates. Bates was a poet and writer. She wrote the words while visiting the Rocky Mountains in Colorado. The song is often sung before sporting events. Its lyrics are:

"O beautiful for spacious skies,

For amber waves of grain,

For purple mountain majesties

Above the fruited plain!

America! America!

God shed His grace on thee

And crown thy good with brotherhood

From sea to shining sea!"

SYMBOLS FROM ★ADVERTISEMENTS★

Some government advertisements have even become symbols. These include:

- Uncle Sam, a man who encourages people to join the army
- Rosie the Riveter, a woman who symbolizes feminism
- Smokey the Bear, a bear who encourages people to take steps to prevent forest fires.

WHAT IS A CELEBRATION?

★ ★

Throwing a graduation cap into the air. Blowing out candles on a birthday cake. Watching fireworks burst into the sky. These images might make you think of special times with family and friends.

A **celebration** is a special occasion. It can be a birthday, holiday, or another event that is special in your life or in the life of someone important to you. These events are often celebrated with the people you love. They might involve special foods, gifts, or activities. They might happen once every year or once in a lifetime.

CULTURAL AND RELIGIOUS CELEBRATIONS

There are many celebrations across the country and around the world. Each culture and religion has its own special celebrations. These celebrations might be celebrated as a community or with extended family. Many of these holidays are marked on calendars. People who move to the U.S. bring celebrations and **traditions** with them.

AMERICAN CELEBRATIONS

There are certain days that are observed as holidays by the U.S. government. These are days that are important to America's history. These holidays help Americans remember their country's past and look forward to its future. Many businesses close on these days so people can spend time with family. Some people do special things to celebrate the importance of these days.

MARTIN LUTHER KING, JR. DAY

★ ★ ★ ★ ★ ★ ★ ★ ★ ★ ★ ★ ★ ★ ★ ★ ★ ★

In 1983, Martin Luther King, Jr. Day became an official U.S. holiday. The country first observed this holiday in 1986. Martin Luther King, Jr. Day is celebrated on the third Monday of each January. On this day, Americans remember Martin Luther King, Jr. who led the campaign for civil rights for Black Americans in the 1960s.

People began celebrating Martin Luther King, Jr. Day as early as 1970. The first celebrations were on January 15, which was Martin Luther King, Jr.'s birthday. People often celebrate Martin Luther King, Jr. Day by attending or taking part in marches or parades.

★ MARTIN LUTHER KING, JR. ★

Martin Luther King, Jr. did many things to improve America. He used non-violent **protests** to help end segregation in the U.S. He helped pass the Civil Rights Act of 1964. This act made it illegal to discriminate against people, or treat people unfairly, because of their race. He also helped pass the Voting Rights Act of 1965. Martin Luther King, Jr. earned the Nobel Peace Prize in 1964. Unfortunately, some people did not like the positive changes he was making. On April 4, 1968, he was **assassinated.**

★ "I HAVE A DREAM" ★

One of the speeches Martin Luther King, Jr. is most famous for is "I Have a Dream". In this speech, he spoke about his dream for his children to "live in a nation where they will not be judged by the color of their skin but by the content of their character". Martin Luther King, Jr. gave this speech in Washington, D.C. during a political rally. The event had between 200,000 and 300,000 people in attendance.

PRESIDENTS' DAY

★ ★ ★ ★ ★ ★ ★ ★ ★ ★ ★ ★ ★ ★ ★ ★ ★ ★ ★ ★

George Washington's birthday has been celebrated in the U.S. since the 1880s. It was celebrated on February 22 until 1968. At that time, the holiday was adjusted so that Abraham Lincoln's birthday could be celebrated at the same time. The holiday was then moved to the third Monday of each February.

Some people celebrate all presidents on Presidents' Day. **Ceremonies** are often held to honor Presidents' Day in Washington, D.C. They are also held in other places around the country.

MOUNT RUSHMORE NATIONAL MEMORIAL DEPICTS U.S. PRESIDENTS GEORGE WASHINGTON, THOMAS JEFFERSON, THEODORE ROOSEVELT AND ABRAHAM LINCOLN

★ GEORGE ★ WASHINGTON

George Washington was the first president of the U.S. He was a part of America's history even before his time as president. George Washington was a commander during the American Revolution. He also helped write the Constitution that set up America's government. As a result, George Washington is sometimes called the "Father of His Country".

★ ABRAHAM LINCOLN ★

Abraham Lincoln was America's 16th president. He is known for leading America during the Civil War. During his presidency, he said, "... this nation, under God, shall have a new birth of freedom—and that government of the people, by the people, for the people, shall not perish from the Earth". He issued the Emancipation Proclamation on January 1, 1863. This freed all slaves held in Confederate states. Abraham Lincoln was assassinated on April 14, 1865.

MEMORIAL DAY

★ ★

The last Monday of every May is known as Memorial Day. Memorial Day began during the American Civil War. In 1864, three women decorated the graves of people they had loved and lost to the Civil War. In 1865, freed slaves and missionaries honored a group of over 200 deceased Union soldiers. As this practice became more common, the holiday, at that time known as Decoration Day, was born. People would spend this day visiting the graves of loved ones killed in the war. They would lay flowers on their loved ones' graves.

MILITARY FLYOVERS HONOR THOSE WHO HAVE LOST THEIR LIVES FIGHTING FOR THE U.S.

After World War I, Memorial Day became a day to honor all U.S. soldiers who died fighting for their country. It is a day to remember the sacrifices these people made and to be grateful for our freedom. People celebrate Memorial Day by holding religious services. They place flags and flowers on the graves of war veterans. A national moment of silence takes place every Memorial Day at 3:00 pm.

ARLINGTON NATIONAL ★ CEMETERY ★

Arlington National Cemetery is part of Memorial Day traditions. It is a national military cemetery located in Arlington, Virginia. Around 16,000 Civil War soldiers are buried there. It is also the home of the Tomb of the Unknown Soldier. This is a **monument** that represents all of the U.S. soldiers who died in war and were not able to be identified. A wreath is placed at the Tomb of the Unknown Soldier every Memorial Day.

SERVICE BRANCHES OF THE U.S. MILITARY

THERE ARE MANY SERVICE BRANCHES OF THE U.S. MILITARY. THESE INCLUDE:

- THE ARMY
- THE MARINE CORPS
- THE NAVY
- THE AIR FORCE
- THE SPACE FORCE
- THE COAST GUARD
- THE NATIONAL GUARD.

A RED POPPY IS SOMETIMES USED AS A SYMBOL FOR MEMORIAL DAY.

JUNETEENTH

★ ★ ★ ★ ★ ★ ★ ★ ★ ★ ★ ★ ★ ★ ★ ★ ★ ★ ★ ★

On June 17, 2021, President Joe Biden signed Juneteenth into law as a federal holiday. However, it has been a Texas state holiday since 1980 and was first celebrated long before then. Juneteenth is a celebration of Black American culture, and of the end of slavery. It is celebrated on June 19 each year.

June 19, 1865 was the first day Black American people in Texas learned about the Emancipation Proclamation which ended slavery in parts of the U.S.

Juneteenth has many names. It is sometimes called Emancipation Day, Freedom Day, or Jubilee Day. The day was first celebrated with prayers, music, and traditional Southern-style soul food. Now, people celebrate Juneteenth with festivals, family gatherings, and religious services.

THE EMANCIPATION PROCLAMATION

President Abraham Lincoln made the Emancipation Proclamation on January 1, 1863. However, Union troops did not arrive to make sure all slaves had been freed in Texas until after the war had been won. This was two and a half years after the proclamation was made.

★ OPAL LEE ★

Opal Lee is considered the "Grandmother of Juneteenth". In September 2016, at the age of 89, she started walking from her home in Fort Worth, Texas to Washington, D.C. She arrived in Washington, D.C. in January of 2017. In the years since, she has held a two and a half mile walking campaign. The two and a half miles represents the two and a half years it took for slaves to learn about the Emancipation Proclamation that freed them. In 2020, Opal Lee started a petition to make Juneteenth a national holiday. Over one million people signed. Opal Lee has been nominated for the Nobel Peace Prize and continues her work today.

INDEPENDENCE DAY

★ ★

On July 4, 1776, the Declaration of Independence was passed. Before declaring independence, American colonists felt they were being treated unfairly by the British government. They did not feel they had the rights that they deserved. The Declaration of Independence said that America was breaking free from British rule to become its own country.

Early Independence Day celebrations included bonfires, parades, and the firing of cannons. Independence Day became a federal holiday in 1870. Today, Americans celebrate Independence Day by getting together with family and friends. They go to parades. They have barbeques or picnics. Many people watch fireworks at night.

FIREWORKS

Fireworks have been used in celebrations around the world since the 12th century or earlier. The first Independence Day fireworks took place on July 4, 1777. This was one year after the Declaration of Independence was passed. Fireworks have been used to celebrate Independence Day ever since. Americans spend about $1 billion on fireworks every July 4.

THE DECLARATION OF ★ INDEPENDENCE ★

The Declaration of Independence was written by Thomas Jefferson with help from John Adams, Benjamin Franklin, Roger Sherman, and Robert Livingston. The Continental Congress voted on the Declaration of Independence on July 2, 1776. Two days later, it was approved. John Adams wrote to his wife that the Declaration of Independence would "be celebrated, by succeeding Generations, as the great anniversary Festival".

LABOR DAY

★ ★

In 1882, a **labor** union leader named Peter J. McGuire suggested something be done to honor American workers. That September 5, there was a parade. It was sponsored by the Knights of Labor, the first national labor organization in the U.S. Around 10,000 workers took unpaid time off work to march in the parade. The organization decided the first Monday of each September should be celebrated as Labor Day.

Labor Day is still observed on the first Monday of each September. Oregon was the first state to formally recognize the holiday in 1887. Soon after, more states followed suit. Labor Day became a federal holiday on June 28, 1894. Today, people celebrate Labor Day by relaxing and enjoying time with family and friends.

PRESIDENT GROVER CLEVELAND INTRODUCED LABOR DAY.

LABOR UNIONS

Labor unions are organizations meant to protect workers. These organizations work with employers to improve rights and benefits for workers. During the 1800s and early 1900s, there were few, if any, labor laws. People worked in unsafe conditions for long hours. They made very little money. Even young children worked hard jobs, giving them little time to learn. Over time, working conditions in the U.S. improved. Now, only about ten percent of the workforce belongs to a union.

UNIFORM MONDAY ★ HOLIDAY ACT ★

The Uniform Monday Holiday Act was signed on June 28, 1968. It said that Presidents' Day, Memorial Day, and Veteran's Day would always be celebrated on Mondays. This helps people enjoy long weekends together. The act also made Columbus Day a federal holiday.

INDIGENOUS PEOPLES' DAY

★ ★ ★ ★ ★ ★ ★ ★ ★ ★ ★ ★ ★ ★ ★ ★ ★ ★

Indigenous Peoples' Day is a day meant to celebrate the history of Indigenous culture as well as all of the contributions **Indigenous** peoples have made to America. Activists worked for years to make this holiday a reality.

On October 8, 2021, President Joe Biden issued a proclamation. It recognized October 11, 2021 as Indigenous Peoples' Day. President Biden wrote "On Indigenous Peoples' Day, we honor America's first inhabitants and the Tribal Nations that continue to thrive today". Indigenous Peoples' Day was celebrated in different cities and states before 2021, but this was the first time it was federally recognized.

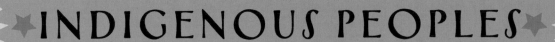

INDIGENOUS PEOPLES

There are over 500 Tribal Nations in the U.S. These are nations of Indigenous Americans and Alaska Natives that can be traced back to America's Indigenous peoples. Around half of these nations are located in Alaska. Each nation governs itself to protect its culture.

COLUMBUS DAY

Columbus Day has only been a federal holiday since 1937. It falls on the same day as Indigenous Peoples' Day. It was created to honor Christopher Columbus, an explorer credited with discovering the Americas. However, many Indigenous people already lived in the Americas at this time. Indigenous people suffered as a result of Columbus's voyage and the many Europeans who followed him. Indigenous nations had their land taken from them, they were forced to change their culture, and many of them died of European diseases or were killed. Many people believe Columbus Day should no longer be celebrated because of the pain that the colonization of America caused for Indigenous nations.

VETERANS DAY

★ ★

In 1919, people celebrated the first anniversary of the end of World War I. They called it Armistice Day. In 1921, it was celebrated again with the burial of an unknown soldier from the war at Arlington National Cemetery. Armistice Day became a national holiday in 1938. Its name was changed to Veterans Day in 1954.

Veterans Day is celebrated on November 11. It is a day meant to honor American soldiers who have served in war. People take time to remember and be grateful for the service of these soldiers. There are ceremonies at the Tomb of the Unknown Soldier. People thank the **veterans** in their life. There are also parades and naturalization ceremonies where veterans and their families become U.S. citizens.

AMERICAN SOLDIERS IN WORLD WAR I

VETERANS DAY CHANGES

An armistice is when the fighting of a war stops because of an agreement between the warring countries. The fighting in World War I ended on November 11, 1918. This is the event that was first celebrated on Armistice Day. However, additional wars took place after World War I. Armistice Day was changed to Veterans Day to honor the people who had fought in all of America's wars instead of just World War I.

SIMILARITIES AND DIFFERENCES WITH MEMORIAL DAY

There are many similarities and differences when comparing Veterans Day with Memorial Day. Both days honor and remember the people who have fought for our country. Both days are a time to be grateful for our freedom and protection. However, Memorial Day is meant to honor soldiers who have died at war. Veterans Day honors all American soldiers, including those who are still living. Soldiers sacrifice many things, including time with their loved ones, to safeguard America and our way of life.

THANKSGIVING

In 1621, a group of English colonists, called the Pilgrims, and the Wampanoag, an Indigenous tribe, shared a feast. Their feast took place in Plymouth, Massachusetts. It included deer, corn, shellfish, and more. As well as sharing a meal, the story goes that the group played games, sang songs, and danced.

Thanksgiving is celebrated on the fourth Thursday of each November to commemorate this event. It became a national holiday in 1863, during the Civil War. Sarah Josepha Hale, the author of "Mary Had a Little Lamb", worked to make this happen. People often celebrate Thanksgiving with their family and friends, enjoying a large meal together. Traditional Thanksgiving foods include turkey, mashed potatoes, and pumpkin pie. Thanksgiving is a time when people reflect on the people and good things they are thankful for. Many people also help others by donating food.

THANKSGIVING DAY PARADES

Parades have been part of the Thanksgiving Day tradition since the early 1900s. The largest Thanksgiving Day parade in America is Macy's Thanksgiving Day Parade, which has been a tradition since 1927. It is held each year in New York City. The Macy's Thanksgiving Day Parade features floats, large floating balloons, and entertainment such as marching bands and singers.

THE WAMPANOAG

The Wampanoag lived in areas of what are now Rhode Island and Massachusetts. Their name means "People of the First Light". While the Wampanoag helped the English colonists, or Pilgrims, who settled near their tribe, they did this in hope of avoiding conflict. Many died from the diseases the Pilgrims brought with them. Over time, much of the Wampanoag land was taken, and their way of life lost. Rather than celebrating Thanksgiving, some of the Wampanoag have a "National Day of Mourning" to honor all their people lost as a result of colonization.

SYMBOLS AND CELEBRATIONS
OF THE FUTURE

★ ★ ★ ★ ★ ★ ★ ★ ★ ★ ★ ★ ★ ★ ★ ★ ★ ★ ★

There are many state and national holidays in the U.S. Many communities have their own special days that celebrate their history and culture. These are celebrated with special foods, music, activities, and more.

What celebrations are most special to you and your family? What do these celebrations mean to you? What are some of your favorite traditions, songs, and foods that come with these celebrations? Reflecting on the celebrations in your life and in America's history can help you learn more about both yourself and your country.

★ OTHER IMPORTANT ★ AMERICAN CELEBRATIONS

There are many important celebrations in America beyond federal holidays. Some of these include:

- Valentine's Day: a holiday in which people share their love for friends and family

- Ramadan: a holy month of fasting for Muslims

- Easter: a Christian religious celebration

- Cinco de Mayo: a holiday celebrating an 1862 battle victory for Mexico

- Halloween: a holiday in which people dress in costume and trick-or-treat for candy

- Diwali/Deepavali: a major religious festival in Hinduism, Jainism, and Sikhism

- Hanukkah: a Jewish religious festival, often called the Festival of Lights, that lasts for eight days

- Christmas: a Christian holiday that many people celebrate by giving gifts

- Kwanzaa: a holiday tied to family and social values, which is celebrated by Black Americans.

★ CELEBRATIONS IN OTHER COUNTRIES ★

Many of America's national holidays are also celebrated in other countries. For example, Thanksgiving is celebrated in Canada on the second Monday in October. Britain, Canada, Australia, and France also honor their veterans on November 11, the same day as America's Veterans Day. Countries around the world celebrate New Year's Day, which is another U.S. federal holiday. Many countries celebrate New Year's Day on January 1, as the U.S. does. Others celebrate at different times, such as China, which has big New Year celebrations, falling on the second new moon after the winter solstice.

GLOSSARY

advertisement
information that appears in media and is intended to persuade people to buy something or vote for a candidate

amendment
a change to a law

assassinate
to kill because of a difference in beliefs

celebration
a special event or occasion

ceremony
a series of actions performed for a special purpose

civil rights
rights to equal treatment and protection by the law, such as in the right to vote

colony
place that is ruled by another country

constitution
a piece of writing that tells the laws of a country

emancipation
gaining political freedom or rights

executive
referring to the branch of government that carries out and enforces laws

federal
national, of the entire country

immigrant
a person who comes to another country to live

independence
the ability to be in control of oneself

indigenous
originally from a place

judicial
referring to the court system in a government

labor
work done to earn money

legislative
referring to the lawmaking body of a government

monument
a stone structure created in honor of a person or event

national anthem
a piece of music that is a symbol of a country and is played at important events

patriotism
pride in one's country

pledge
a promise or agreement

protest
to speak out or show disagreement

represent
to stand for

residence
the place where someone lives

right
a freedom or power to do
something

sculpture
a solid, three-dimensional
representation of something

segregation
the separation of people based on
race or another characteristic

symbol
something that stands for
something else

tradition
an action or belief passed down
through generations

veteran
person who was in the military

INDEX